12/1992

A DECENT CUP OF TEA

After reading this maybe
you can open your own
little tea-room in Nashua —
then we'll have our afternoon tea there —

       Love,
       Mom

Merry Christmas

A DECENT CUP OF TEA

MALACHI MCCORMICK

Clarkson Potter/Publishers
New York

ACKNOWLEDGMENTS

Several people have been very helpful in providing me with research material, and I thank them sincerely: Michael and June von Essen, for the Johan Rohde designs; Leslie Ferrin, of the Ferrin Gallery in Northampton, Massachusetts; Jinny De Paul; Linda Arbuckle; Elaine Bolz; Montgomery; Michael Cohen; Leslie Lee; Garson Pakele.

Published by Clarkson N. Potter, Inc., 201 East 50th Street, New York, New York, 10022. Member of the Crown Publishing Group.

CLARKSON N. POTTER, POTTER and colophon are trademarks of Clarkson N. Potter, Inc.

Manufactured in the United States of America

Library of Congress Cataloging-in-Publication Data
McCormick, Malachi.
A decent cup of tea / by Malachi McCormick.
1. Tea. 2. Cake. I. Title.
TX817.T3M35   1991   91–4182
641.6'372—dc20   CIP

ISBN 0–517–58462–X
10 9 8 7 6 5 4 3 2 1
First Edition

CONTENTS

Introduction 6

A Brief History of Tea Drinking 11

An Introduction to the Types of Tea 24

On Selecting Your Teas 33

The Teapot 39

How to Make a Decent Cup of Tea 43

Good Things to Have with Your Tea 54

A Beginner's Guide to Reading Tea Leaves 68

Out to Tea 76

Some Books About Tea 77

Introduction

In among all the tea books about Limoges and napery, about high or low tea, the kettle-to-the-pot/pot-to-the-kettle books, the intermittent letters to the *Times* from self-styled Anglophiles discoursing on the class aspects of the High Tea, the Meat Tea, Afternoon Tea, the Tea Tea, and what have you—there is, I suspect, room for a Fanfare to a Decent Cup of Tea book, a Tranquil Tea book, a Plain(er) Tea, which is my own particular tea bent.

I am no expert in consumer affairs—except that I am a modest consumer—but it seems to me that the tea consumer gets some pretty bad breaks from a tea industry that often obfuscates and blinds with fake elegance and puffery about "Special Blends," instead of educating (which some of the smaller companies attempt to do), and that more than doubles the price of tea by putting it in tea bags.

Similarly with the serving of our preferred beverage: could not restaurants be as diligent in providing us with as decent a cup of China as they do Java? Look at the expense that is lavished on coffee-brewing equipment. All we need for tea is a simple kettle and pot, and a selection of four or five teas (at least for a start; we will consolidate our grasp later!).

HOW THIS BOOK CAME ABOUT

I suppose, in one sense, that this book began the moment I first left Ireland to live in London, more than thirty years ago. Contrary to the Hub of the Empire's reputation for Definitive Tea, I encountered the shock of insipid, lukewarm tea at every level of public tea drinking.

I was working at the time for J. Lyons & Company—the very same company responsible for the famous Lyons Tea. And yet the tea dispensed from the Lyons tea trolleys, which at 11:00 A.M. and 3:00 P.M.

were wheeled through office and factory alike at the J. Lyons HQ, Cadby Hall—the very Vatican of Tea—and drunk by employees at every level, seemed to me to be always lacking in some way. Either it tasted stewed or it was deathly warm or it had a metallic edge; it was too weak or too strong, too bitter or too sweet, too milky or—worst of all—not milky enough. In a word, watery!

It was a parody of tea! It was a mockery!

It was in London, too, that I first encountered the tea bag, which at the time was no more than a pernicious encapsulator of fannings and tea dust, designed purely to extend the tea importer's already substantial profits by using up the large amounts of both that were left at the bottom of tea chests after the larger leaf grades had been taken out for packing.

In those days, I took tea in places high and low, and each one had its own special way of spoiling tea. In fact, the only place where I could feel sure of getting a really Decent Cup was at Lyons famous Tea Shops. Here the tea was, it seemed, invariably made and dispensed by matronly women who invariably called me "ducks."

After many years and much peregrination, when I finally came to live in New York I discovered that it was as difficult to get a Decent Cup in the former colony as it had been in the former Hub of the Empire. In New York, coffee reigned supreme, and its exciting aroma propositioned me on every street corner, while tea was available only as the same uninviting weak, watery, warmish brew I had first encountered in London.

Things, it was true, were pretty bad all over. But it came as a real shock to hear my mother complain about the state of tea in Ireland. Other nations might fall, but—I would say to myself—never Ireland! In my mind's eye I saw my grandmother, Boadicea-like, repel the hordes with her battle cry: "When I makes tay, I makes tay!" Now, here was my mother telling me such stories as being served—on the Dublin-Cork train!—a warm liquid in a plastic container. After one baffled sip she found herself asking the waiter, "Is this tea or coffee?"

If there was one single moment of conception for this book, that was it! Enough, I heard a voice say; take your pen and set down, for the generations to come, the simple facts of tea. I cannot now remember if the words "A light unto the nations" were used, but I had no doubt about the commission I was receiving. At that very point, The Decent Cup of Tea movement was born.

A BRIEF HISTORY OF TEA DRINKING

The origins of tea drinking are lost in the steamy vapors of prehistory. When, we inquire, was cup of amber brew first raised to lip? Who pronounced, at the breakfast of time, the first benediction, "It is good" (long since abbreviated, but with no loss of respect, to the protracted "Aah!")?

And how did tea drinking come into being? Was it a conscious, deliberate process, a matter-of-fact "I think, finally, I'll put on some tea"? Or was it, like penicillin, one of those felicitous discoveries? We construct a possible scenario: "What is this liquid here? Hmmm, tastes ... interesting. Actually, it tastes rather good!" And at this stage our Archimedes of Tea leaps out of his bath and runs proclaiming into the marketplace.

As with most such questions, it is not history but myth that supplies the answer. One ancient Chinese myth tells us that it was the emperor Shen Nung who discovered the revered brew in 2737 B.C. One day, we are told, the good emperor was watching a kettle of water being boiled for his supper when some leaves from a nearby tree fell into the boiling water.

(A kettle without a lid, we note. And what, we might inquire, was water being boiled for, if tea had not already been invented?) We will not ask such questions, because we are not churls or curmudgeons. But I, for one, am curious to know how fresh green leaves, boiled in water, could produce a drink remarkable to an emperor, when anybody with any sense would have simply skimmed off the leaves.

Myth requires willing accomplices, and so we will be charmed by the story and the image. Why shouldn't Shen Nung be the one? If a roomful of monkeys randomly poking the keys of word processors could—as has been theorized—reproduce the entire works of Shakespeare, it is but a simple process to invent tea by rigorously observing and tasting the effects of the random falling of leaves into unlidded kettles containing liquids of different temperatures.

Here we will shamelessly employ the clichéd device of the lazy recorder: "And the rest is beverage history!" More accurately, it's beverage myth.

A widely held alternative version in the Orient (which ignores some well-established chronologies) ties the discovery of tea to the birth and spread of Buddhism, some two thousand years later. Ta Mo, or the Bohdidharma, was a blue-eyed Indian prince; after converting, he went on to become a Buddhist saint. Ta Mo believed that perfection resulted from endless contemplation, and he meditated for many years without sleep. Once, though, in the middle of meditating, our hero — to his deep disgust — fell asleep. (If you feel a myth in the offing, dear reader, you are right.) To ensure wakefulness, the chagrined saint cut off his eyelids and threw them to the ground, whereupon they immediately took root and grew miraculously into tea plants. And so today, thanks to Ta Mo, we lesser beings have the stimulus of tea to ensure wakefulness.

It is apparently the lot of the missionary to be ignorant of indigenous wisdom. Had Ta Mo inquired, any Taoist in China could have told him of the three great crimes of Taoism: the false education of the young, the uncritical admiration of bad paintings, and the wasting of good tea. And as a bonus saved him that painful business with the eyelids.

It must be said that tea scholarship favors the Shen Nung story over the Ta Mo tale, mainly because it fits with established data. Confucius certainly drank tea in the 5th century B.C.: the philosopher Yen Ying mentions it. Around A.D. 800, Lu Yu wrote the *Ch'a Ching* (The Classic Book of Tea). Most of what Lu Yu had to say about tea applies as much today as it did then, and his writing is pervaded by a quiet, almost religious reverence for his subject. For Lu, the most important thing about tea was that it should be taken "in an atmosphere of tranquility."

By this time all of China had switched to tea, or the Jade Queen, as it was reverentially referred to.

Lu Yu and his colleagues wrestled with some of the knotty questions of the new religion. What was the correct attitude to the taking of the sacrament — restraint or indulgence? Lu Yu advised: "For exquisite freshness and vibrant fragrance, limit the number of cups to three." An anonymous poet thought seven cups would do it, to "render a feeling of tranquility . . . tea will drive the doctor away and make you feel strong; tea will add to your years, and the enjoyment of your longevity."

In the classic tradition, each succeeding dynasty in China sought to outdo its predecessor. And tea was an obvious arena. The Tangs (A.D. 617–907) favored tea compacted into brick form, so the Sungs (960–1280) introduced the very opposite, powdered tea; this in turn gave way to the cured leaves of the Mings (1368–1644). The pendulum had swung to both extremes and settled in the middle. And that's pretty much the way it's been ever since.

By the eighth century, China had become the greatest and most powerful empire in the world, already trading extensively with Japan, to the east, and with countries as far west as Persia. The Japanese soon became avid tea drinkers, and themselves quickly developed the famous

Tea Ceremony, which sought then, as it still pretends today, to surround the simple acts of making and serving tea with an etiquette of real and aesthetic grace.

This led to many other refinements: one example is that extraordinary branch of Japanese architecture, the Sukiya, or tea room. We cannot read Okakura Kakuzo's account of the tea room in *The Book of Tea* and not feel that there is something very special going on here:

The tea room is unimpressive in appearance. It is smaller than the smallest of Japanese houses, while the materials used in its construction are intended to give the suggestion of refined poverty. Yet we must remember that all this is the result of profound artistic forethought, and that the details have been worked out with care perhaps even greater than that expended on the building of the richest palaces and temples. A good tea room is more costly than an ordinary mansion, for the selection of its materials, as well as its workmanship, requires immense care and precision.

How extraordinary that tea would inspire such high ideals and such asceticism! It is a remarkable property of tea that it seems to bring out the best in us, something at once spiritual and profoundly human. It is hard to imagine the same happening with any of our other beverages: wine, beer, water, coffee, spirits — not to mention the extended (and often feuding) family of colas!

Though tea reached Persia early on, it did not seep farther west until the beginning of the seventeenth century. And then it was not the English but the Dutch, with their famous East India Company, who introduced it, with the Portuguese coming in a close second.

Oddly enough, Marco Polo makes no mention of tea, though he must surely have encountered it in the court of Kublai

Khan. In fact, the first mention of tea in the West is in the book *Voyages and Travels* by the Venetian Giambattista Ramusio, who heard about this Chinese tea from Hajji Mahommed, a Persian merchant. That was in 1559. Giambattista didn't know it then, but tea would play a significant part in the economic downfall of Venice, with the discovery of the great sea routes.

Soon after this, a succession of Jesuit missionaries in China made mention of tea in their letters home. One of them, the extraordinary Matteo Ricci of memory palace fame, went into considerable detail and was himself convinced that tea was the source of Chinese longevity and vigor. Another observed that the Chinese honored a guest by serving tea, but the proffering of a third cup was a hint that it was time to leave.

In 1595, a Dutch navigator sailing for the Portuguese, Jan Hugo van Lin-Schooten, published an account of his travels in the Orient, in which he so engagingly described Japanese tea customs that the Dutch immediately dispatched four ships to Java. In 1602, the Dutch East India Company was set up. In 1610, according to company records, the very first Chinese and Japanese teas were shipped from Java to Europe. Very soon, the merchants of Holland were writing to Java to make sure there was some of both on every ship sailing west!

The French and Germans got their first tastes of tea from Holland. The German experience proved the briefest of flirtations; they soon reverted to their great love, beer. Tea created more of a splash among the French, but they soon returned to wine.

In about 1653, an English admiral found a small amount of tea in the galley of a Dutch ship he had captured, and it is thought that this could be the first tea to arrive in England. Four years later, some Dutch tea was put up for auction at Garway's Coffee House in London (coffee had

reached England twenty years before).
And on September 25, 1660, the great
diarist Samuel Pepys entered: "And afterward I did send for a cup of tee (a China
drink) of which I never had drank before,
and went away."

The New Amsterdamers apparently
were drinking tea in lower Manhattan before it arrived in England. Later, after the
city became New York, tea gardens were
built in imitation of the London pleasure
gardens, and street vendors sold spring
water for tea making.

From this time forward, many great
tea-related historic events and develop-
ments took place. The British East India
Company rose and fell. Taxes on tea raised
money for all sorts of enterprises; William
of Orange's 1690 victory at the Battle of
the Boyne was thus financed. The Boston
Tea Party was only one of many anti-
tea-tax measures along the Atlantic coast
that sparked the American War of Inde-
pendence. The clipper ships of the mid-

nineteenth century raced back with their cargoes of teas because the first of the new harvest commanded premium prices.

Several attempts were made to introduce tea plantations to the United States. In 1775, a French botanist, André Michaux, tried near Charleston, South Carolina, but was soon recalled to France. In 1848, Dr. Junius Smith tried it again in the same area, but this too ended in failure. In 1858, the U.S. government sent Robert Fortune, a horticulturist, to China for seeds of *Camellia sinensis,* and these were later given out free to planters in the South. Some bushes grew in the Carolinas, Georgia, Florida, Louisiana, and Tennessee, but there was no commercial production. Further unsuccessful attempts were made between 1890 and 1920, but one way or another, the aspiration to market an American-grown tea has persisted in that area of the country.

The latest incarnation of this aspiration is the Charleston Tea Plantation, situ-

ated on an old Lipton's Tea experimental plantation in Charleston. When I spoke to Mack Fleming, one of the partners of this enterprise, he was enthusiastic about their brand, American Classic Tea. It is marketed as "The only tea grown in America." He sent me some samples — tea bags, but packets of loose tea are planned. Industry opinion felt that high labor costs would price any American tea out of the market, but ingenuity at the plantation has developed a mechanical harvester that promises to overcome this problem. One wonders, though, how discriminating a machine can be in its plucking.

I opened my box of American Classic Tea. The brightly colored packet, sporting the Stars and Stripes and bearing the copy "A noble cup — proud of its exotic past and native heritage — ready to claim its rightful place as one of the world's great teas," makes a patriotic appeal to the red-blooded, but I have to report that the brew, to my taste, lacked body and pungency.

AN INTRODUCTION TO THE TYPES OF TEA

For several years now I have been buying my tea at the Porto Rico Importing Company, a charming and unpretentious old store (founded in 1907) on Bleecker Street in New York City's Greenwich Village. Big burlap bags bulging with coffee beans crowd the floor like broad-beamed dancers in a Reginald Marsh nightclub scene; large clear glass jars of loose teas sedately line the shelves.

At first all the teas look the same: blackish, dried, slightly dusty leaves. But examination reveals large differences. In

one jar, the tea leaves are tiny, uniform in size, and black with a tinge of reddish brown. In another, they are large, coarser, with variegated colors—deep sienna brown with flecks of bisque. Another has small dried flowers mixed in. Another seems a dark olive green, its leaves tightly knurled in intriguing little balls. And on and on.

One of the many reasons I like the Porto Rico shop is that I can see the teas, which are not shut away in packages that drip unctuously with the swirling calligraphy of fake elegance, or want to cheer me up with their Peter Max bell-bottomed with-itness.

At Porto Rico, large white plain letters on the jars show the names of the teas. Many, such as Lapsang Crocodile, Earl Grey, Darjeeling First Flush, Russian Caravan, Jasmine, and Iron Goddess of Mercy (why does this tea make me think of Margaret Thatcher?), sound mysterious, exotic—and daunting to a newcomer.

Which, of course, is why so many people confine themselves to buying familiar tea bags and remain unaware of the existence of the long tradition, fine quality, and extraordinary diversity and deliciousness of tea.

So let us take a demystifying look at some tea essentials: how and where it grows, how it is processed, how it gets to us, how it is properly made, and so on.

Perhaps the most extraordinary fact about tea, considering the many shelves of glass jars of the different varieties at my store, is that all tea comes from one evergreen shrub, *Camellia sinensis,* with its dark green leaves and fragrant white blossoms.

But in the cycle from seed to tea leaf, many factors come into play that affect the taste and the look of the end product. *Camellia sinensis* grows in many different parts of the world and, obviously, the differing qualities of the soil, intensity of the sun, the rainfall, and other aspects of climate have a major bearing. For example, in moist tropical lowlands, leaves grow profusely and quickly, and the tea packers will harvest leaves every two weeks. But the tea from the same bush will grow much more slowly where it is cooler — say, at an altitude of four thousand feet. It will be harvested every six weeks, but it will be more highly prized for its characterful taste, as we see with some of the Darjeelings.

Left to its own devices, uncultivated, *C. sinensis* would grow into a tree thirty to forty feet high. (There is an eight-hundred-year-old tea tree in Yunnan province that is sixty feet high.) But cultivated tea is kept pruned to a height of three to three and a half feet, for two important reasons. First, pruning stimulates the growth of young leaves (considered best for tea); and second, the low height makes harvesting the leaves easier.

Obviously, the degree of pruning is another factor, as is the decision of when to pluck the tea. But another factor is what to pluck. Superior tea comes from the tiny shoots of new tea leaves and the thin unopened buds; the quality lessens, the bigger the leaves that are plucked. Again, great room exists for variation in quality, and not every tea manufacturer might be able to resist bulking up the harvest.

Good tea plucking is a demanding job. Traditionally it has been done by women, who select and pick the leaves and buds and drop them into baskets, which are transported from the growing area to a nearby "factory." The next stage in the process is "manufacturing."

At this point the tea is changed from its just-plucked state to one of its final forms: black, green, and oolong tea.

BLACK TEA

Black teas come mostly from China and India. The process for "manufacturing" black tea, which is fermented, is the most complex of the three forms. The plucked leaves are subjected to withering, rolling, roll breaking, fermentation, firing, and grading. These were once done by hand, but today much of bulk tea manufacturing is mechanized.

Withering: The leaves are placed on large trays to dry out for a period of less than a day. The leaves become limp.

Rolling and roll breaking: The limp leaves are subjected to a mechanical rotating process. This causes heat and oxidation, which brings out the oils that give the distinctive taste, and gives the leaves their familiar twisted look. Oddly enough, the twist of the leaves affects taste also, because it affects infusion time, which directly affects flavor and pungency.

Fermentation: The rolled leaves are spread out on a surface for several hours to ferment, when they develop a rather startling copper color. The degree of fermentation directly determines the flavor, concentration, body, and color of the tea and the pungency of the tannin, which is reduced as fermentation progresses.

Firing: Fermentation is halted and bacteria and enzymes in the tea are destroyed with a blast of dry hot air. The heat must be carefully controlled, as the residual moisture content of the leaves determines taste and quality.

Grading: After passing through all these stages, the tea is a mixture of broken and unbroken, large and small leaves, which need to be sifted in sieves and graded—mostly for commercial reasons.

All black tea is graded by size, and only by size. Quality is not implied, except that it is easier to inspect larger leaves.

The names and characteristics of the whole-leaf grades are: *Orange Pekoe*—long, wiry, twisted leaves, occasionally with yellow tip and bud leaf; *Pekoe*—small, tightly rolled leaves; *Souchong*—large, coarse leaves.

The broken-leaf grades are: *Broken Orange Pekoe* (known as "BOP" in the trade)—small leaves, often with yellow tip and bud leaf. This grade is frequently used as the main ingredient in blended teas; *Broken Pekoe* (BP) — slightly larger than Broken Orange Pekoe, often used as a filler in blended teas; *Broken Pekoe Souchong* — somewhat larger than Broken Pekoe and also used as filler; *Fannings* — much smaller than Broken Orange Pekoe, a quick brew; *Dust* — the smallest, a very quick brew, much used in catering.

These grades, with some variations, apply to all black teas hailing from India, Sri Lanka, China, Java, and Sumatra.

GREEN TEA

The basic characteristic of green tea is that it is unfermented, which gives it a taste that, to my mind, is gentler, subtler, more natural (in the sense of being less processed) than black teas. Gunpowder Tea, so named because of its granular appearance, is probably the best-known green tea in the West.

The leaves for green tea are not withered (which in fact starts the fermentation process for black tea) but steamed. Then they are rolled and fired until the leaves are properly dry and twisted. Grading follows.

Green teas come mainly from China and Japan, where they are very highly regarded. Many cultivators go to extraordinary lengths to ensure perfection in the crop, some even to the extent of massaging the leaves individually. But green tea does not enjoy the same following in the West—at least, not yet.

OOLONG TEA

Oolong teas are partially fermented, combining the qualities of black and green tea, and are grown mainly in China and Taiwan.

ON SELECTING YOUR TEAS

I am now assuming that you wish to turn your back quite definitely on the world of mass-market tea bags, and so offer some thoughts that might prove helpful.

Most people start with a black tea, as opposed to green or oolong teas. If you have drunk tea in the past, the odds are in favor of its having been black tea, because most tea is black tea.

There are many high-quality black teas available, at very reasonable prices, such as Darjeelings, Assams, Keemuns,

Ceylons. Lapsang Souchong is a smoky black Chinese tea that I am partial to, but it is not to everyone's taste. Green teas and oolongs are milder teas, more natural-tasting, some say, that make for very pleasant sipping. You might have had green tea at a Japanese restaurant.

I have been accused of being snobbishly anti–herbal teas. This is not true. I am very partial to some herbal infusions, particularly chamomile and rose hip. There is, however, something of an academic argument about whether they are teas or infusions. I suppose that if I have an opinion on the subject it is that the teas that come from *Camellia sinensis* and go through the black-green-oolong curing process constitute a recognizable family, and that a distinction between teas and herbal infusions is useful.

Let it be said again that fine tea is one of the world's last remaining bargains. One may drink the very finest of teas for literally pennies a cup. At the Porto Rico

Importing Company, the most expensive tea, the wonderful Darjeeling Vintage Himalaya, costs twenty dollars a pound, which at 200 to 250 cups to the pound works out to something less than ten cents a cup. And you can buy as little as a quarter of a pound of any tea. So you will not, and should not, be restrained by price in your explorations.

Let me do a little comparison shopping for you: the tea in twenty tea bags of very ordinary tea has a net weight of about 1.5 ounces and sells for $2.00 to $2.50. This is about $22 to $27 a pound. We will not listen to the tea packagers who tells us they have to pay all the little men who put the tea in the little bags.

By all accounts the tea bag was an American invention, dating back to the early 1900s. Of course, then they weren't tea bags in the way we know them now: a tea supplier sent out samples of new teas in little silk bags. In post–World War II England the tea bag made its first appearance in the catering world, in hospitals, factory canteens, and "institutions" — an inauspicious beginning, to be sure. And a properly defensive tea industry has been rationalizing tea bags ever since.

Last year in London I came across a full-page advertisement in the *Times* for the latest improvement to the tea bag. It was now, the tea company trumpeted, "round"! Oh yes, that's what's been missing all along: we all crave that quintessential quality of roundness, and we spot its absence in a trice.

As the reader will gather, when it comes to the controversy of loose tea *v.* tea bags, I fall squarely on the loose side of the fence, for a complex of reasons that have to do with considerations of taste, flavor, aesthetics, simplicity, and resistance to marketing, commercial convenience, and extra profit. If those reasons are insufficient, I will grant that there may also be some sheer and unalloyed prejudice in there as well (though I will admit that when loose tea is not available, I will drink tea-bag tea without too much whining). But why should we settle for less, especially when it costs more? Tea-bag tea is safe tea. Make mine loose.

Do yourself a favor and get to a loose-tea shop. Or send off for mail-order catalogues and order by mail. Here are four mail-order places that sell fine teas:

Harney & Sons, Ltd.
P.O. Box 676
Salisbury, Connecticut 06068

Porto Rico Importing Company
201 Bleecker Street
New York, New York 10012

Schapira Coffee Company
117 West 10th Street
New York, New York 10011

Zingerman's Delicatessen
422 Detroit Street
Ann Arbor, Michigan 48104

My personal inclination is toward un-blended teas. A blended tea means at best that others are imposing their tastes on you. The giant tea packers — whose blends, incidentally, sometimes comprise as many as twenty-five different teas — say that the main reason for blending is to achieve consistency of taste, which to my mind is utter hogwash. Try to imagine blended wine. Or cheese.

The real reasons for tea blending are that, in a changing market where availability and price fluctuate, sometimes wildly, the packer can maintain price and profit by switching some teas for others without the customer's detecting it. It's just another sad example of the exploitation of the innocent, and therefore uncomplaining, consumer.

So please, get yourself some decent tea. And save yourself some money into the bargain. And if you like, you can blend your own teas.

THE
TEAPOT

Human ingenuity is a source of endless fascination. It has also been a source of endless teapots, many of them fascinating, many of them serviceable, and some of them both. I thought a few pointers on picking out a decent teapot might be of use.

First, be sure to pick up the pot to try it out. You should be able to use the handle without burning your hand (this is probably the most frequent fault in teapot design). The handle should feel well balanced and comfortable to the hand.

Obviously, you will probably have to imagine the pot filled with boiling water to gauge this. In the same way, you should imagine whether the weight of a full pot will be comfortable for you.

Another point to be aware of is that certain teapots will transfer their heat very rapidly to the handle. Many metal teapots tend to do this, and some ceramic ones do too. Because of this, you may find the handle insulated with raffia, which can look attractive. The question to ask, however, is "Is it effective?" Be sure to inquire.

The top of the spout of the pot should come up to the same level as the top of the pot, so that the pot can be filled up. This may seem like an obvious point, but in teapot design it is oft honored in the breach.

A teapot should have a deep, snugly fitting lid—perhaps with a lip—with no threat of falling out during pouring. And the lid should have a reasonably sized knob on the top so you can easily put the lid on and take it off.

As you will see when we get to the recommended method of making the Decent Cup, two points that are essential have ramifications for the design of the teapot:

The hotter the tea the better.

Because of the unpleasantness of too much tannin in the tea, which comes out after about five minutes of infusing, it is important to separate the tea liquid from the tea leaves after about five minutes. This is a primary rule of the Decent Cup. Teapot design and tea-making procedure have sought to accommodate this fact, and the result is that you have options to consider and choices to make.

You would do best to choose a teapot that has a built-in perforated strainer at the base of the spout, to keep the leaves in the pot. (Seek to get only one cup per person from the pot; any "refill" should come from a freshly made pot.) Alternatively, you can use a tea strainer. Yet another option is a mesh tea infuser or a tea ball. (These you would withdraw from the teapot after the five-minute infusion time.)

I favor the teapot/external tea strainer combination, a personal preference that has further relevance, discusssed in the chapter on reading leaves.

I will not engage the question of which material is best, as that is so much a matter of taste.

This said, pick a pot that you like and will be comfortable with. Be prepared to pick it out with at least as much thought as you would give the selection of a new spring jacket. This is a pot that you will become as attached to, almost, as you would to a cat.

In fact, you would probably do well to pick out two teapots, one large, to fill the needs of several tea drinkers at once, the second one smaller, for yourself.

HOW TO MAKE A DECENT CUP OF TEA

When first I broached this subject in a miniature book of the same title, I received a letter from a teacher of English in Ann Arbor, Michigan. My correspondent asked, quite snippily, if I didn't mean "How to make a cup of decent tea."

How could I explain to her that she was *absolutely* right and *totally* wrong all at once? Real life doesn't always parse. When we call out "Who's there?" in the dark, we are reassured by the answer "It's me." Do we know anybody who says "It is I"? Our friend from Ann Arbor could correct the grammar of all Ireland, but it still wouldn't scan. Over there, the standard unit of acceptable tea *is* the Decent Cup of Tea, not the Cup of Decent Tea.

Most people like the title. They understand it. They know, from long experience, that there's something desperately accurate about the word *decent* here. Imbued with the scaled-down, cut-back expectations that go with retaining sanity in our world, it also carries something of a last appeal. Once, before the fall, there was magnificent tea; now, all we're asking for is a decent cup. Is that too much to ask?

Apparently, most tea drinkers think it is too much to expect that one will get a decent cup of tea outside of one's own home—except, perhaps, in the home of a trusted tea-drinking friend.

This has to change. This *will* change. We will spread the word. We will police—politely, affably, but determinedly—those

institutions that proffer tea to the masses,

demanding that they serve us, not better, but right! (Note to Ann Arbor: I know, I know.) We will inspect premises. We will barge into kitchens. We will wheedle wiretap permission from sympathetic judges who haven't had a Decent Cup themselves for years. What shall we call ourselves? Total Tea! Tea Now! The Amber Party! The Friends of the Leaf! Those of us with access to religious-tract printing plants out there in Missouri and Ohio will have our little leaflets printed up after hours, and we will pass them out on the streets, at airports and bus stations, and on ferries. It has even been said (by Nostradamus, if I'm not wrong) that a great Tea Drinker will arise in the year 2000, and will, in that millennial sea change, bear up in a rapture all those who in their hearts have proclaimed the words "I would do anything for a decent cup of tea." Yes, dear Friends of the Leaf, anything, including fight. Not for the principles, but for the tea.

Of course, we have principles too, the

principles that have sustained tea drinkers over the centuries. So I've taken this time to sketch out our program for the decade. The mere purchase and perusal of this book, and repetition of the words "I would do anything for a Decent Cup of Tea," automatically place you on active reserve. We will be in touch.

Obviously, such an ambitious program of proselytism requires that our own house be in order. Which is why we review the rules of proper tea making here.

We assume that all the requirements are at hand. I will list these here and take the opportunity to explain a few related points at the same time. You will need:

Some proper loose tea of choice, kept in a proper container, or tea caddy, usually tin or wooden. The word *caddy* comes from the Malay word *kati*, a unit of weight (1⅛ pounds) that tea was sold by. In time it came to mean the wooden box that a *kati* of tea came in. One may buy tea in caddies, which do very well for ongoing storage.

But, like other items of equipage, the caddy has been raised to exquisite levels.

Some cold water, fresh from the tap, in a kettle or other heating container. The amount of water should be sufficient for scalding as well as drinking purposes. I recommend tap water, though local quality may drive some to seek alternatives.

A container, such as a teapot, in which to make the tea.

A cup from which to drink the tea. Some people insist on using china and swear that tea doesn't taste anything as good out of anything else. I routinely drink my tea from a large mug—I like a large amount of tea—but I do admire the art and elegance of a fine tea service.

A teapot with a strainer in the spout, or a separate strainer, metal or bamboo, which you place over the cup as you pour.

A variety of wire-mesh-strainer containers are available, which hold loose tea and are placed in the pot. They have the advantage of being extractable later, when the tea is ready. If you use one, make sure it is big enough to allow for the expansion of the tea leaves, which is quite considerable. I don't use them myself, basically because I think they are not necessary and therefore a little fussy. Good tea tends to sink to the bottom of the pot, in any event; and I have no objection to the occasional appearance of a few leaves in my tea. Indeed, their presence is absolutely necessary if you want your fortune told.

Sundry items of tea equipage found in some elegant tea services, such as slop bowls, spoon boats, sugar tongs, and so on, are often desirable optional extras. But — and I want to be clear — they are *not* essential. One can go most of one's life without finding out how a spoon boat is steered. I have endured some terrible tea from the best of equipage in my day, and I have had many memorable cups where the equipage was Battered Utilitarian Improvisational. When I trained as a lab chemist at Irish Steel in Cork Harbor, we made our tea in glass beakers heated on Bunsen burners. I had tea in the galley of a trawler off the coast of Kerry; the huge black kettle sang its song on a turf fire, and the tea in an old cracked mug never tasted better. I've had glorious tea in monastery kitchens, one reassuring pleasure of the flesh that the monks had not forsworn. And in the middle of haymaking in County Tipperary, Mrs. Ryan brought us a billycan of tea through the fields at noon, with the milk and sugar already in; we drank it down, sitting in the shade, our backs up against the newly made hayrick, and couldn't imagine anything better in the whole world.

You may desire additives—milk, sugar, honey, lemon, singly or in combination, to taste. Of course, one may take tea with no additives at all, and many who would call themselves purists insist that it is the only way.

But there is another reality. For centuries, many different peoples have taken tea with milk, presumably for no better conscious reason than that they preferred it that way. But now research suggests that something more may have been going on, something that Diane Ackerman, in her fine book *A Natural History of the Senses*, terms "this self-protective yen." Here's what she has to say about tea with milk: "Tea contains a lot of tannin, which is toxic and can cause cancer, but milk protein reacts with tannin in a protective way, preventing the body from absorbing it." No doubt this will not be the last word on the subject, but I know that, to my taste, both milk and sweetening are important, though I will do without both when I taste a new tea.

Let us also settle the question, Which has more caffeine, tea or coffee? While tea has a higher content than coffee, in the brewing almost three times as much caffeine is extracted from coffee as from tea.

And now, finally, how to make a Decent Cup of Tea.

Run sufficient fresh, cold tap water into a kettle or other container, and bring the water to a full, rolling boil.

Pour about a cup of boiling water into your teapot. Put the kettle back on the heat to keep it boiling. Swirl the water in the pot to heat it, then throw out the water. Put about a teaspoon of tea per person into the pot, and immediately pour on the boiling water.

When it comes to measuring the right amount of tea, many tea manuals call for "a teaspoon for each person, and one for the pot." In my view, that "one for the pot" often produces too strong a brew, but you should experiment and make up your own mind. Since many tea manuals have been published by tea companies, there may well be other reasons for their encouragement of our lavishness.

Now stir the leaves (they should sink to the bottom), replace the teapot lid, cover the pot with a tea cozy, and let the tea infuse. The infusion time depends on the type of tea, and will vary from about three to six minutes. Set a timer.

(The moment when boiling water touches tea has been called "the agony of the leaves." This sadistic little anthropomorphism keeps cropping up in books about tea, but it ill befits us as Friends of the Leaf.)

During infusion, two things happen: the flavor of the leaves comes out, and the tannin is released. A certain amount of tannin adds to the flavor of tea, but too much will overpower it and make the tea bitter and undrinkable. The time for best flavor and optimum tannin is about five minutes. But, as in all matters of taste, experimentation is in order.

Pour the tea immediately, using a strainer if desired. Because of the tannin, one should not attempt to get a refill cup from the pot. For seconds and thirds, make a fresh pot. To facilitate this, you may wish to put the kettle on again, ahead of time.

Drink the tea unadulterated, or add

milk, sugar, honey, or lemon to taste.

Note: Besides the use of good tea and the strict control of infusion time, the most important thing about making a Decent Cup of Tea is that the minimum of heat be lost from the time the water boils to the time the tea is drunk. This is the reason for scalding the teapot and using the tea cozy. Placing the teapot on a warm surface is also a big help.

To these I have added my own refinement, which is always to boil extra water and to heat the cups or mugs with it at the same time that I wet the tea in the pot. I also invented—in my mind—the lidded tea mug. Then I noticed that Chinese stores sell lidded tea mugs, and presumably have done so for years.

Then I invented the tea stein! If the stein lid keeps the flies out of beer, it can keep tea heat in. And with a flick of my thumb, I swig. Copyright that!

GOOD THINGS TO HAVE WITH YOUR TEA

I have already indicated a strong preference for plainer fare at teatime. I consider clotted cream as being too much for tea. And though I am partial to the odd cream pastry, I do regard these as being coffee rather than tea fare.

The small sandwiches served as a first course at teatime are appropriate and tasty, but the tendency toward elaborate, multi-ingredient sandwiches — right up to the stuffed deli style — is in my opinion contrary to the spirit of afternoon tea. Afternoon tea is primarily a social occasion, not a meal, and food served should be light. It is not normally intended as a replacement for dinner.

In a changing world, it is folly for anyone to try to impose old concepts of mealtimes, types, and sizes. But we would do well to recognize that each old system had its own wisdom, and common sense about food is important to good health. There is an old Irish proverb: "Follow steadfastly the ways of your ancestors."

One of the things we are forced to concede is that afternoon tea is today very much a sometime thing—who can afford the time?—but it is all the more welcome because of that. By the same token, however, I especially recommend making the effort to participate more than rarely, if only to demonstrate to ourselves that there are more important things in our lives than business and money. Or at least as important. This is the philosophical, spiritual side of teatime: it is something we do with and for our friends. Which is another reason why food should not be central.

Let us be careful, however, to steer clear of the severe Puritan ethic, which would probably banish as frivolous the very concept of afternoon tea. I was recently invited to tea by a friend who is quite steeped in tea lore. As a delicacy she served quail eggs, which she had gone out of her way to get for me. The eggs were delicious, but long after the taste faded, her gesture remained in my mind as special.

On a more practical, even technical level, I advise against the use of strong-tasting fish in fish-based sandwiches. Delicious as they are, they tend to overpower the tea. The odd anchovy butter or salmon mayonnaise, though, is the traditional exception.

As a consequence of the foregoing, all the recipes that I give here tend to be on the traditional side and tend to be available for the classic Irish afternoon tea.

BUTTERMILK SCONES

These days, scones seem to occupy a special place in the hierarchy of teatime fare, and rightly so. Nothing could be simpler to prepare, and nothing taken with tea equals a hot scone spread with butter and strawberry jam. Which is why afternoon tea at home is so hard to beat.

There are many different kinds of scones, but these are particular favorites of mine.

2 teaspoons baking powder	2½ cups unbleached all-purpose flour
1 cup buttermilk	1 teaspoon salt

Preheat the oven to 400° F.

Dissolve the baking powder in a little of the buttermilk. Mix the flour and the remaining buttermilk together, using a wooden spoon. Then add the salt and the baking powder solution. Mix thoroughly.

Roll out the dough on a floured board and cut into scones about 2 inches in diameter. Place on a lightly greased baking sheet and bake for 15 minutes, until lightly browned. Split the scones, spread with lashings of butter, and serve hot.

Makes 12 to 16 scones

TEA BRACK

This very popular commodity at teatime is something more than a fruit loaf and something less than a full-blown cake. It is indescribably delicious — thinly sliced, served plain or lightly buttered. It was always featured, home-baked, of course, by my mother when a sense of occasion demanded it, and I thought it was one of the most delicious things I ever tasted. I still do.

3 cups golden raisins	Grated rind of 1 lemon
3 cups dark raisins	
2 cups firmly packed light brown sugar	1 teaspoon freshly grated nutmeg
1 cup cold breakfast tea	1 teaspoon freshly grated allspice
½ cup Irish whiskey	1 tablespoon honey, dissolved in a little warm water, for glazing
4 cups unbleached all-purpose flour	
3 eggs, beaten	
3 teaspoons baking powder	

Put the raisins, sugar, tea, and whiskey in a large bowl. Cover it and let this soak together overnight, or for about 12 hours.

Preheat the oven to 300° F.

Add the flour, eggs, baking powder, lemon rind, and spices to the raisin mixture. Mix very well with a wooden spoon. Put the mixture in a greased 10-inch round cake pan and bake for 90 minutes, until nicely browned. When done, remove from the pan and let cool on a wire rack. When cooled, brush the brack with the warm honey mixture, for a mouth-watering shiny glaze.

Makes one 10-inch cake

MALTED FRUIT LOAF

American visitors to Europe tend to be overwhelmed by the extraordinary range of high-quality breads and cakes to be found in bakery shops. And it has been my experience, conversely, that Europeans visiting the United States issue a constant ululation about our bread.

One of the things that catches our eyes — and our palates — when we go to Ireland and Britain is the ubiquitous little malted fruit loaf, packaged in colorful wax paper. It is ubiquitous because everyone loves a slice or two — plain, buttered, or toasted, with or without jam — with their tea. I have no doubt that it is the intriguing malt taste that does it.

1½ cups milk

2 tablespoons unsalted butter

2 tablespoons light brown sugar

½ teaspoon salt

3 tablespoons malt extract

2 cups unbleached all-purpose flour

2 teaspoons baking powder

½ teaspoon baking soda

3 tablespoons golden raisins

1 tablespoon chopped lemon peel

3 tablespoons currants

1 tablespoon honey, dissolved in 3 tablespoons warm water, for glazing

Preheat the oven to 375° F.

Warm the milk in the top of a double boiler. Add the butter, sugar, and salt, and stir until these are dissolved. Then let the milk mixture cool to a comfortable warm. Stir in the malt, a little at a time, to get a uniform mixture.

Mix the flour, baking powder, and baking soda in a large bowl. Add the raisins, lemon peel, and currants. Mix well. Now add the milk mixture, and stir well with a wooden spoon until it's very smooth.

Spoon the mixture into a greased medium-sized loaf pan and bake. Check for doneness (a knife will come out clean) after 35 minutes; it may take an extra 5 minutes after that.

Turn off the oven, take the loaf out, and brush the top with the honey glaze. Then put it back in the oven for about 5 minutes.

Take it out of the oven. Turn it out on a wire rack to cool.

Makes 1 loaf

CRUMPETS

Crumpets are classic tea fare. They can be cooked in an oven, but they seem to come off a griddle hotter and tastier, somewhat more of a crumpet. The trademark holes become tiny reservoirs of melted butter. With an overlay of jam or preserves, these are very hard to beat, though definitely on the squishy side.

4	eggs	1	cup milk
3	tablespoons sugar	2	cups unbleached all-purpose flour

Separate the eggs. Beat the whites until stiff, and the yolks until smooth and lemon-colored. Add the sugar to the yolks, stir in well, and then add the milk, again stirring well. To this mixture gradually add the flour, beating well all the while. Finally, stir in the beaten egg whites. This needs to be a fairly thick batter, so you may need to add a little more flour. Cover the batter and let it stand for an hour.

Heat a griddle — preferably over a gas flame (though the ideal would be an open fire) — or a heavy frying pan. Using a large spoon, drop about ¼ cup of the mixture onto the hot surface of the griddle and let it cook for about 4 minutes, or until it is lightly browned; turn over and brown lightly on the other side. Serve quickly.

Makes about 15 crumpets

DUNDEE CAKE

This is a popular teatime fruitcake, rich but still quite light.

Grated rind of 1 large orange

1 cup sugar

½ pound (2 sticks) unsalted butter, softened

4 eggs, lightly beaten

2 cups cake flour

1 teaspoon baking powder

Pinch of salt

½ cup chopped blanched almonds

½ cup golden raisins

½ cup raisins

½ cup dried currants

½ cup chopped mixed candied peel

Juice of half an orange

¼ cup blanched almonds, for garnish

Preheat the oven to 300° F.

Grease a 9-inch round cake pan, and line with wax paper. Bruise the orange rind with the sugar. Add to the butter and beat. Gradually beat in the eggs.

In another bowl, sift together the flour, baking powder, and salt. Add the chopped almonds, raisins, currants, and peel. Stir in the butter and sugar, then the orange juice.

When well mixed, spoon into the cake pan. Add the blanched almonds in a close-fitting pattern all over the top.

Put in the oven and bake for 2 hours, or until a skewer stuck into the center of the cake comes out clean.

Makes 1 cake

LEMON POPPY SEED CAKE

This classic Victorian cake, a variation on the pound cake, has made a big comeback in the last few years in the U.S., where I first encountered it. For tang and texture, it's hard to beat.

½ cup black poppy seeds

½ cup milk

¾ pound (3 sticks) unsalted butter, softened

1½ cups granulated sugar

Grated rind of 2 large lemons

8 large eggs, separated

2 cups cake flour

½ teaspoon salt

SYRUP

¼ cup confectioners' sugar

Juice of two large lemons

Put the poppy seeds in the milk to soak for 2 hours, then drain and rinse in a fine sieve under the cold tap.

Preheat the oven to 350° F. Grease and flour a 10-inch tube pan.

With a wooden spoon, cream the butter; then slowly add 1 cup of the granulated sugar, beating in well. Add the poppy seeds; beat in well. Add the grated lemon rind; beat in well. Now add the egg yolks, one by one, beating each one in well. The mixture must be very light.

Beat the egg whites in a large bowl until they peak. Add the remaining granulated sugar and beat until stiff peaks form. Sift the flour and salt together; add slowly to the egg yolk mixture, folding in all the while. Then add the beaten egg white very gradually, again folding in all the while.

Pour the batter into the tube pan and bake for an hour, or until a knife comes out clean when inserted.

While the cake is baking, make the syrup by dissolving the confectioners' sugar in the lemon juice. As soon as the cake is baked, prick it all over with a fine-tined fork or a skewer, then pour the syrup all over the top. Let it cool, slice, and serve.

Makes one 10-inch cake

65

CLASSIC AFTERNOON TEA
SANDWICHES

Tea sandwiches call for day-old, thinly sliced, square white loaves. Cut off the crusts and butter the bread sparingly, using soft butter so the slices don't break. Add a modest amount of filling, and no more; two tablespoons per slice of any of the salad fillings below is sufficient.

Spread the filling, add any garnish, and place another slice on top. Using a long sharp knife, make an X-cut to get four small triangular sandwiches. Place the cut sandwiches on a serving platter, and cover with a damp napkin.

Here are some favorite fillings of mine, but be inventive.

Slices of hard-cooked egg: With a sprinkling of snipped chives.

Egg salad: Mix chopped hard-cooked eggs with some mayonnaise; add salt and pepper and a good pinch of snipped chives.

Egg salad with capers: Add a tablespoon of chopped capers in place of the chives.

Egg salad with cayenne and cumin: To your basic egg salad add a small pinch of cayenne and two small pinches of cumin.

Fresh tomato slices: With a sprinkle of chives, freshly ground black pepper, and salt.

Tomato slices with basil: With a sprinkling of salt.

Cucumber: Use the long, greenhouse variety, peeled and thinly sliced.

Mustard cress: Leaves only.

Shrimp salad: Boil, shell, and chop some shrimp. Add mayonnaise and pepper and salt to taste. Sprinkle on a little snipped dill.

Anchovy butter and Greek olives: Combine 1 ounce of anchovy fillets, 2 tablespoons of butter, and a pinch of black pepper in a small food processor. Spread *very* thinly on the bread, and add a layer of finely sliced pitted Greek olives on top.

Crab mayonnaise: Make this as you would the shrimp salad—just add some chopped parsley and lemon juice.

Salmon mayonnaise: Again, follow the notes on shrimp salad, using good-quality, well-drained canned salmon and a nice amount of dill.

Boiled chicken and ham: Thinly sliced, with Coleman's mustard.

Wood-smoked ham: With chutney.

Avocado slices: With Dijon mustard dressing and chives.

A BEGINNER'S GUIDE TO READING TEA LEAVES

One ought to be able to sit quietly and read a simple book on tea without being asked to wrestle with questions of theological and cosmological import. Nevertheless, dear reader, that is what I am going to ask you to do now.

My mother, who includes reading the leaves among her many talents, casts a practiced eye over the leaves in my cup. It is an eye that penetrates porcelain, through the cup, into the soul.

"I see two people, one more mature, one less so. One is straining to harmonize, to achieve cooperation, but it's a pretty one-sided cooperation, if you ask me." She says some more, and concludes with one of her trademarks, a good-humored fatalistic bark of a laugh, which she got from *her* mother. She employs this laugh a lot when she listens to politicians on television.

I immediately recognize the two people in her commentary. I am the "mature one," the other is my daughter, and I contemplate her observation for a while. Later on, however, it suddenly strikes me that she might have been alluding to our own relationship.

It was a nice example of a basic rule of good leaf reading: the reader provides the framework, the skeleton, which the subjects flesh out themselves. "Oh, there's the journey!" was another of her allusions. There is no doubt in my mind which one she meant.

A tea-leaf reading by a good practitioner has something of a Rorschach test to it, with the reader guiding the subject gently along the road. But it more often is a mere parlor game.

Ireland in the 1920s and '30s was a country awash with political and religious passions, which both my parents wished to avoid. As a result, "common sense" was enshrined in our home.

But while my father's metropolitan Dublin background perhaps made that easier for him, my mother's rural roots embraced certain arcana. Divination was one of them. Crops, the weather, betrothals, marriages, the outcome of a horse race—there was an abiding interest in the future. She couldn't deal a hand of cards for whist without commenting on the love or the money it presaged.

As a young lad I had heard my mother from time to time allude to a tea-leaf-reading event that had somewhat traumatized her. In a casual reading for a visiting friend, my mother saw something very dark in her afternoon cup. Within the week her friend's husband was dead (in a car accident, as I remember it). The incident had a chilling effect on my mother, who refused to read the cups for years afterward.

How to Prepare for a Reading

Obviously, since leaves are of the essence in this reading of our future, you must use a teapot without a strainer—and, of course, loose tea. That means *positively no tea bags!* Indeed, we should right now posit the disturbing question, If we use tea bags, can we be said to have a future?

A larger-leafed tea makes for better readings. The classic teacup, wider at the mouth, tapered at the bottom, is preferable, as is a white or light-colored interior without a pattern. The surfaces of some cups are dimpled or fluted or otherwise irregular in shape; these are unsuitable, as they impede the free swirling of the leaves that precedes reading. Mugs (too deep, too straight-walled) are also difficult swirlers, and therefore unsuitable.

Make, pour, and drink the tea in the usual way, but make sure to leave a teaspoon or two of tea. While drinking, the subject should reflect on a question of significance, something he or she wishes to know about.

After drinking the tea, the subject swirls the teacup by the handle. Some say to use your "non-pen" hand, and to swirl it away from you three times. After swirling, turn the cup upside down in the saucer, letting the tea and whatever leaves may fall into it. The reader picks up the cup and turns it the right way up.

When the reader looks into such a cup, it is said that he or she is looking into the world, the soul, the future of the subject. It is a world with a particular structure. The patterns of leaves all have more significance or less. Those patterns and clusters nearest the rim of the cup relate to the very near future, while those farther down relate to the more distant future. Leaves at the very bottom relate to the very distant future. Also, the position of the subject in this universe is represented by the handle of the cup, and the closeness or oppositeness of the leaves to the handle will have their own significance in relation to the subject.

The first impression from the overall disposition of leaves, or from a particular cluster that takes the immediate attention of the reader, is said to relate to the question of significance that the subject wants information on, and is often the first order of business in the commentary. Conversely, it is sometimes kept till last, perhaps with an eye to dramatic effect.

We tend to think of the particulars of our lives as being special, without precedent. But the wise and practiced reader has seen it all before, many times, and knows that our lives break down into a handful of categories: we want to know about our loves; our fears, dreams, and dreads; our successes and failures; our desires; our health; our fortunes and misfortunes. Our changes. Our decisions. But, though the wise reader has seen it all before, to him or her each subject is still unique.

The good reader is open, observant, and imaginative—and will interpret the overall picture, rather than recite obvious or crude symbols, the "faces in the fire." This is not to deny clear symbols. An anchor or airplane will very likely signify a journey; a heart, love; a ring, marriage; a star, good luck; a bridge, transition; a snake or dagger or gun, danger; and so on.

Order, clarity, freedom, motion, confusion, strength, weakness, closeness, distance, attitude—all are very often suggested in a cup. Clusters may represent individuals, and the cluster nearest the handle often represents the subject. A truly good reader lets what comes come and explores the meaning of things he or she is "getting" from the images and feelings perceived.

A reading is not a contest in which the subject sits back, waiting for the reader to guess how much money he or she has. A good reader will often draw the reader in and use this participation to go further along in the examination.

The mechanics of tea-leaf reading are not too difficult to learn, given the tutelage of a good practitioner, but there aren't too many of them about. A good way to start is to read your own cup on a regular basis. Use your imagination. You will be surprised at how quickly you will be able to notice and interpret patterns, and your own knowledge of yourself should serve as an effective check.

One more thing: good readers never charge for their services. Avoid anyone who does! But it is perfectly proper for a subject to express appreciation with a gift, monetary or otherwise.

Out to Tea

There was a time when going out to after-noon tea, or meeting a friend for tea at a tearoom or hotel, was just about one of the nicest things one could do. Today, there are signs that afternoon tea is attempting a comeback, a trend very much to be en-couraged. Hotels and tearooms are re-discovering the lucrative slot of "teatime" and have begun to reinstate it, the older hotels in those magnificent spaces, at once comfortable and grand, and the tearooms in the cozier, intimate, even quirky spaces that are often their special charm.

I am drawn to the more rumbustious rooms, where the fare is good, proper, affordable, and unpretentious, and where one may strike up a conversation with a stranger as easily as with a friend. (For me, Bewleys in Dublin fits this description per-fectly; and there, incidentally, with an ex-emplary beverage ecumenicism, we find both excellent tea and the finest coffee, democratically dispensed.) I object to the antitea attitudes of many cafés, which spare no expense on their neon-lit hissing and spluttering coffee machines and offer fifty different coffee preparations, but regard tea-bag tea as sufficient. Perhaps now we can educate them.

The pace of our lives hardly permits the regular taking of afternoon tea, but the same pace demands that we make time for tea from time to time — if only to remind ourselves of who's in charge.

Some Books About Tea

No book about tea could consider itself complete if it did not say something about books about tea. And there are many of them: a few stand out.

The first is *The Classic Book of Tea,* by Lu Yu, to which I referred in the chapter on history. It was translated by Francis Ross Carpenter, and published by Little, Brown & Co., Boston, in 1974.

Next comes the classic *Book of Tea,* by Okakura Kakuzo, reprinted by various publishers (my copy is from Tuttle). First published in 1906, it gives an extraordinary look into the Japanese soul.

5,000 Years of Tea, by Derek Maitland, published in 1982 by Gallery Books in New York, is an excellently researched and nicely illustrated book on the history and practice of tea. A slight demur—the book is overly Anglocentric. It reminds me of teenagers who, upon discovering sex, feel they have invented it. But that's a minor quibble; this is a really fine book on the subject.

The last book I will recommend to your attention here is *The Book of Coffee & Tea: A Guide to the Appreciation of Fine Coffees, Teas, and Herbal Beverages,* by Joel, David, and Karl Schapira (first published in 1975 by St. Martin's Press). This is a book that, despite the misplaced priorities of its title, really tells us about tea on many different levels. The authors come from a

family that have been tea and coffee merchants in New York since 1903, and they
are steeped in tea and tea lore.

I will leave you, dear reader, with a
thought that the Schapira's share with us in
their book. They say:

Don't hurry. When making tea you have
only time. Let tea be a refuge, a genuine
change of pace. Brewing your tea is part
of drinking it and drinking it part of
your life. Let the tea gently stimulate
you to reflect on how the smallest part
touches and is touched by the infinite.

About the Author

Malachi McCormick is the author of *Malachi McCormick's Irish Country Cooking* and *Cat Tales*. He lives on Staten Island, New York, and is the founder of the Stone Street Press, which specializes in handcrafted books.